ESL Stories for Preschool

Book 1

5 Bonus lesson plans
and 35 flashcards
to download from
TeachingEnglishGames.Com

SHELLEY ANN VERNON

CONTENTS
5 Stories and 52 Colour Illustrations

STORY ONE - I'M HUNGRY

Here comes an ant.

(Hup 2, 3, 4,
Keep it up!)

"Hello Ant.
How are you?"

"I'm fine
thanks,"
said Ant.

Here comes a spider.

(*Itsy bitsy ditsy witsy*)

"Hello ant," said the spider.

"Hello spider," said the ant, "how are you?"

"I'm fine thanks," said the spider, "but I'm hungry. I am going to eat you. Yum yum yum!"

Here comes a snake.

(Sssssssssssssssssssssss)

"Hello spider," said the snake.

"Hello snake,"
said the spider,
"how are you?"

"I'm fine thanks,"
said the snake,
"but I'm hungry.

I am going to eat you.
Yum yum yum!"

Here comes a bird.

(Whoooooosh)

"Hello snake,"
said the bird.

"Hello bird,"
said the snake,
"how are you?"

"I'm fine thanks,"
said the bird,
"but I'm hungry.
I am going to
eat you.
Yum yum yum!"

Here comes a cat.

(*Meow)*

"Hello bird,"
said the cat.

"Hello cat,"
said the bird,
"how are you?"

"I'm fine thanks,"
said the cat,
"but I'm hungry.

I am going
to eat you.
Yum yum yum!"

Here comes a fox.

(silent stealthy gestures)

"Hello cat,"
said the fox.

"Hello fox,"
said the cat,
"how are you?"

"I'm fine thanks,"
said the fox,
"but I'm hungry.
I am going to
eat you.
Yum yum yum!"

Here comes a lion.

(*Roar)*

"Hello fox,"
said the lion.

"Hello lion,"
said the fox,
"how are you?"

"I'm fine thanks,"
said the lion,
"but I'm hungry.

I am going
to eat you.
Yum yum yum!"

I'm Hungry Lesson Plan

All stories have activities such as the ones below included via PDF download along with all the vocabulary flashcards to print and use in classroom games. Also included are PDF versions of the story illustrations which may be shown on a screen and printed if desired and more.

Why are the activites, colouring, flashcards and extras separate as a download and not included in this book? Because the book would be twice as thick and cost twice as much. This is significant because the book is printed in full colour. Bear in mind that all the downloadable extras are free, I included them to give you as much help as possible, at no extra cost.

Key vocabulary & picture flashcards provided by PDF download

Animals: Ant, spider, snake, bird, cat, fox and lion.

Greeting: Hello how are you? I'm fine thanks.

Verbs: eat

Phrases: I'm hungry, I am going to eat you.

Pre-story activities

1. Listening games for the first three animals

Introduce the first three animals and play Run and Touch. Tell the children to run over to the picture as if they were the animal you name. You will have to make up what you think and ant and a spider sound like! For the spider they could pretend to be like spider man and fire their web at the correct picture from their wrist and then fly through the air to that picture. Next play Show Me variation 3. You will find all games mentioned here in the ESL Games for Preschoolers Learning English available on Amazon.

2. Greetings

Now that you have given the children some practice understanding the first three animals, introduce the greetings. Seat the children in a circle and take a ball. Ask the whole group, "Hello, how are you?" and have the group answer back with, "I'm fine thanks." Have the children repeat this back to you three or four times in unison. Now roll the ball to one child and say, "Hello, how are you?" Help the child reply to you with, "I'm fine, thanks". The child rolls the ball back to you and you repeat with each child. It's best to only do this with a group of 8 or it gets boring. With a bigger group put the children into pairs in the circle. Seat the two in a pair close together and have them hold hands, then leave a clear gap between the next pair. Now roll the ball to a pair of children and they can reply together, which cuts down the whole exercise by half.

If this is your very first session with the children see the games book introduction for suggestions for the first lesson. Alternatively use the above idea but if children are reluctant to respond to you let them do a thumbs up while you say "I'm fine thanks!" Once the children get used to you and become less shy they will be happier to speak English.

Remember it's a lot to take in getting to know you and having a first ever lesson in English so be gentle and don't insist on a response.

3. More listening games and the rest of the animals

Next introduce the remaining four animals and play some more listening games. For example, tell the children to mime being the different animals. Then play All Change, either with the four new animals or with all seven animals together if your children can manage it.

As soon as the children understand the different animals read the story. However you can of course play speaking games where the children name the animals before you read the story if you prefer.

Ideas to use during the story

As each animal arrives on the scene make the appropriate noises for that animal and have your children gradually take over with the sound effects. Use hand gestures where appropriate such as moving your fingers and hand to imitate a spider.

When your children are ready, pause and allow them to name the animal instead of you. For example you say, "Here comes a …" and pause to give the children a chance to name the animal. After a few weeks and after you have told the story a few times, pause after "Here", and encourage the children to join in with you saying the whole sentence, "Here comes an ant".

Use this technique in all the stories but if it is slow to elicit the words or phrases do not do it throughout the whole story – just for certain key elements, so that the story telling process remains relatively fluent and so that you do not make a meal of it.

Useful feedback from a teacher

'My students still LOVE this story. I usually do a second bit at the end where I look sad and say POOR ANT, POOR SPIDER when they get eaten and then at the end I get them to pretend to sprinkle pepper on first the lion who goes A A A A TCHOOOOOOOOOOO! and then out comes the fox etc. They love that and they are all happy that the animals get out. The very little ones (2 - 3 year old children) love this one too.'

Post-story activities

1. Version of British Bulldog

Here's a setting for British Bulldog that fits with the story. All the children start at one side of the room and they are ants. One child is in the middle who is a spider. You say, "go ants, go!" and the ants run to the other side of the room. The child in the middle must try to touch one of the ants. Then you either have two spiders in the middle or switch animals and the one who has been touched becomes a snake, while all the other children become spiders. Repeat until you have gone through all the animals.

In this game keep an eye any bigger children who may become rough on the smaller ones in their excitement, and make sure that the same child is not caught each time – just rig the game in any way you think of to avoid this. For example hold that child's hand and take them down the end to safety, or just tell the child in the middle that they can catch any child except a particular child, or group of children.

Another way around this is to simply name the next child who will go in the middle. For example if the same child has been caught twice say, "well done, now it's Jacky's turn in the middle because Celina has already had a go".

2. Colouring

For a quiet activity after an excitable one like British Bulldog above, give out black and white pictures and let the children cut out the animals and colour them in for 5 minutes. These are included with the bonus downloads provided with this book.

3. Listening games

Play Musical Statues but tell the children mime the different animals you name as they move about the room. Play Hop Bunny Hop but use the animals from the story. Alternate with a quiet game such as animal bingo. Bingo cards are provided which you use in combination with the small coloured flashcards.

4. Speaking games

Using the animal vocabulary from the story play Stepping Stones, or The Crossing. Let a child pick out an animal picture, secretly look at it and then mime that animal. The other children have to guess which animal it is. Other speaking games are Three Cups or even Snap if you print off enough picture flashcards and deal them out amongst the children.

Access the lesson plans in your book owner download area.

Example of more advanced level of text

All stories come with a more advanced level of text, available in the free download section.
Here is an extract for I'm Hungry

Picture 7

Here comes a lion. ***Roar***
"Hello fox," said the lion.
"Hello lion", said the fox, "how are you?"

"I'm fine thanks," said the lion.

"What are you doing?"

"I'm out looking for food because I'm hungry. And look, I've found some. Unfortunately it's you!"

And the lion gobbled up the fox, with the cat, the bird, the snake, the spider and the ant inside. Yummy!

Then the lion felt queasy. He felt a hiccup coming on. Hic! Out popped the fox. Hic! Out popped the cat. Hic! Out popped the bird. Hic! Out popped the snake. Hic! Out popped the spider. Hic! Out popped the ant!

"Is everyone OK?" asked the ant? "Yes, we're fine thanks!"

Example of black and white colouring included with the free downloads

STORY TWO - ANNA AT THE ZOO

Anna and her daddy are at the zoo.

At the zoo Anna sees one snake. There he is. One snake.

At the zoo Anna sees two elephants. There they are, two elephants. One, two.

At the zoo Anna sees three ponies. There they are, three ponies. One, two, three.

At the zoo Anna sees four giraffes. There they are, four giraffes. One, two, three, four.

At the zoo Anna sees five bears. There they are, five bears. One, two, three, four, five.

At the zoo Anna sees six ducks. There they are, six ducks. One, two, three, four, five, six.

At the zoo Anna sees seven lions. There they are, seven lions.
One, two, three, four, five, six, seven.

At the zoo Anna sees eight monkeys. There they are, eight monkeys. One, two, three, four, five, six, seven, eight.

At the zoo Anna sees nine birds. There they are, nine birds. One, two, three, four, five, six, seven, eight, nine.

At the zoo Anna sees ten fish. There they are, ten fish. One two, three, four, five, six, seven, eight, nine, ten!

Then Anna and her Daddy have an ice cream and go home.

STORY THREE - ARCHIE AND HIS PONY

Here is Archie on his pony. He is going to jump ten jumps.

Here is jump number one. It is a purple jump. Archie jumps it. Over he goes! Yippee!

Here is jump number two. It is a green jump. Archie jumps it.
Over he goes! Yippee!

Here is jump number three. It is a red jump. Archie jumps it.
Over he goes! Yippee!

Here is jump number four. It is a brown jump. Archie jumps it. Over he goes! Yippee!

Here is jump number five. It's a black jump. Archie jumps it. Over he goes! Yippee!

Here's jump number six. It's a water jump, and it's blue. Pony stops to have a drink.

Archie shouts "Naughty pony! (thwack) GO pony GO!!!!!!"

Ouch! Pony FLIES over the jump. Over he goes! Yikes!

Here is jump number seven. It is a pink jump. Archie jumps it.
Over he goes! Yippee!

Here are jumps number eight and nine. They are yellow jumps.
Archie jumps them. Over he goes! Yippee!

Here is jump number ten. It is an orange jump. Archie jumps it.
Over he goes! Yippee!

Steady pony! Stop stop stooooooooooooooop!

Archie, you did ten jumps! Here's a rosette. Well done Archie, well done pony!

STORY FOUR - HIDE AND SEEK

"Hello Bird.
How are you?"

"Hello Giraffe,
I'm fine thanks.
How are you?"

"I'm fine thanks.
Let's play hide and
seek."

"Yes let's," said Bird.

"Bird, you hide
first", said the
giraffe.

"OK, Giraffe, count
to ten", said the bird,
and it flies off to
hide.

Giraffe counts to ten while bird hides.

One, two, three, four, five, six, seven, eight, nine, ten!

(The children cover their eyes and count with you)

"OK Bird, is that you on the yellow path?"

"No, it's me the spider."

"OK Bird, is that you behind the green bush?"

"No, it's me the monkey."

"OK Bird, is that you in the blue pond?

"No, it's me the snake."

"OK Bird, is that you in the green grass?

"No, it's me the lion."

"OK Bird, is that you in the red flowers?

"No, it's me the bee."

"Where are you?

Where are you?

Where are you?!!?

OK Bird, is that you…"

"…on my head! There you are!"

"Well done Bird", said giraffe, "now I'm going to hide."

"OK giraffe, but, erm, aren't you a bit big to hide?" said the bird.

STORY FIVE - THE MARCHING ANTS

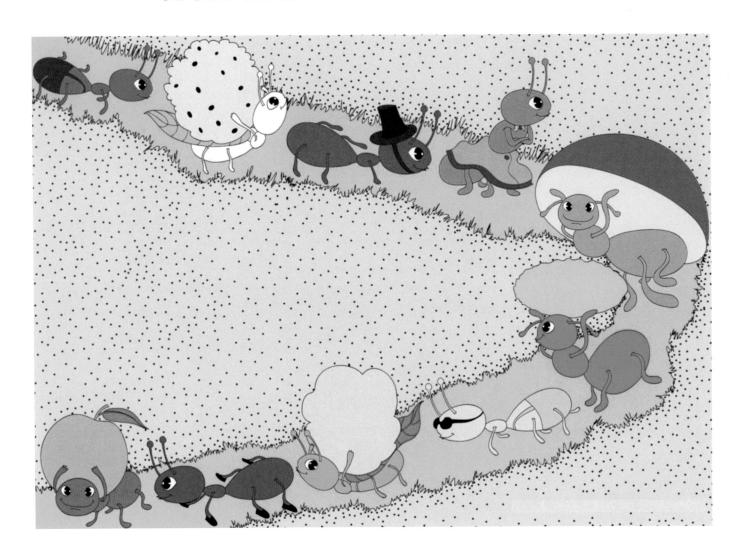

Ten little ants are marching down a path.
Up two three four, keep it up!

The purple ant feels tired, and falls asleep under a white flower. And now there are only...nine little ants marching down a path.

The white ant feels tired and falls asleep under a brown bush. And now there are only...eight little ants marching down a path.

The red ant feels tired and falls asleep under some orange flowers.
And now there are only...seven little ants marching down a path.

The orange ant feels tired and falls asleep under a red flower. And now there are only...six little ants marching down a path.

The pink ant feels tired, and falls asleep in the yellow grass. And now there are only...five little ants marching down a path.

The blue ant feels tired and falls asleep in some pink flowers. And now there are only...four little ants marching down a path.

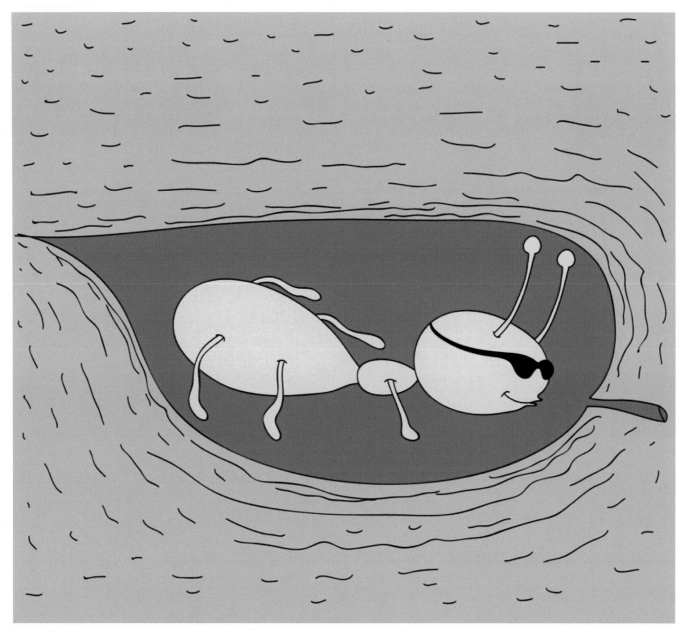

The yellow ant feels tired and falls asleep in a blue pond. And now there are only...three little ants marching down a path.

The green ant feels tired and falls asleep in a green garden. And now there are only...two little ants marching down a path.

The black ant feels tired and falls asleep in a purple bed, with his teddy bear. Now there is only one little ant marching down a path.

The brown ant feels tired and falls asleep in a green field. Good night.

SONGS TO GO WITH THESE STORIES

Available as CD or Download on:
www.teachingenglishgames.com/eslsongs.htm
And Amazon

16 Life-size downloadable masks to cut out and wear for role-plays
Black and white masks to colour

ACCESS TO DOWNLOADS

Five lesson plans with games and activities to teach the language and vocabulary in these stories are included as a free download with this paperback.

Also included are flashcards in small-size, A5 and A4, a bingo set and extra colouring, all available to download online.

When printing it is recommended to use 180 or 200-gram card so that your flashcards are not see-through when placed upside down.

It is recommended that you cover the flashcards with sticky plastic that can be purchased in rolls at stationary shops. Sticky back plastic is better than laminating pouches as it is cheaper, lighter to carry around and has soft edges. The flashcards do not quite as professional as laminated ones but are just as hard-wearing.

The small-sized flashcards may be used with the bingo sets and with table top games or games where you need multiple flashcards in small groups.

The A4 flashcards are for use in classroom games as described in the lesson plan for this story book and in the preschool and primary games books.

Flashcards for these stories are:

1. ant	10. bear	18. flower	25. red
2. spider	11. duck	19. grass	26. white
3. snake	12. elephant	20. path	27. yellow
4. bird	13. fish	21. pond	28. blue
5. cat	14. giraffe	22. garden	29. black
6. fox	15. bed	23. teddy bear	30. brown
7. lion	16. bushes	24. pink	31. green
8. pony	17. fly	25. purple	32. orange
9. monkey	18. field	26. grey	

Please email Shelley on info@teachingenglishgames.com to access the flashcards and print them for yourself.

ABOUT THE AUTHOR

Following her BA degree in languages at Durham University, England in 1989 Shelley Vernon took a TEFL qualification and became a teacher. She taught in language schools in the UK and privately around the world for several years.

She created resources based on her experiences and has shared her ideas with thousands of teachers around the world, bringing enthusiasm and a love of learning into the classroom, as well as great results. Shelley's approach concentrates on enhancing listening and speaking skills through language games which involve repetition and through fluency activities which have genuine communicative value rather than artificial conversation.

In addition to her degree in foreign languages, Shelley holds a university degree in music (2000) from Canterbury Christchurch College. She loves classical music, and enjoys keeping fit with skiing, yoga and walking her adorable cocker spaniel. She also writes songs and has 3 preschool songs CDs. She speaks occasionally at conferences. (IATEFL Cardiff 2009 and YALS Belgrade 2011, UCN, Hjorring, Denmark and Barcelona 'Exams Catalunya' in November 2015.)

Shelley Ann Vernon's resources are available on Amazon US and Europe in paperback and PDF download on www.TeachingEnglishGames.com. Please email Shelley for details on info@teachingenglishgames.com. These resources include:

1. 20 stories for preschool beginners aged 3 to 5 or 6.
2. 10 stories for special days in the year, including this Halloween story.
3. Stories for primary school children.
4. ESL Games for Preschool and Teaching Twos Report.
5. 3 sets of songs on CD or download version including a songs activity book with CD1 and masks of the story characters to cut out and colour with pre-coloured masks to wear when acting out the story, the song or for role-plays.
6. 176 English Language Games for Children: A book of classroom games for primary children that is a good compliment to the stories where you have larger classes or young primary aged children. For smaller groups of preschoolers the ESL preschool games book is more appropriate.
7. Teach Your Child English: A book of games for one to one use including three online video demonstrations of lessons in progress.
8. 30 Fun ESL Role-Plays and Skits: Book of easy role-plays for children for use one on one and in small groups.
9. ESL Classroom Activities for Teens and Adults

Made in the USA
Monee, IL
04 August 2022

10898382R00038